"THER
FR

Limericks from Around and About Alberta

by Jim Elliott

NOSE CREEK EDITIONS

Calgary, Alberta

*****

ISBN 0-921057-66-0

First Printing: February 8, 1999

Publishing by NOSE CREEK EDITIONS

708 Lake Ontario Drive S.E.

Calgary, AB, Canada T2J 3J8

Telephone (403) 271-9123

*****

1. Limericks. 2. Alberta–Poetry
I. "There Once Was a Man from Alberta..."
PS8559.L5453T53 1999 C811'.54 C99-910229-X
PR9199.3.E439T53 1999

FOR

This work is dedicated to the fine people of Rockyford, who fed me a sandwich and who allowed me to shelter in their beer parlour (even though I was not of legal drinking age) during the devastating virtual nuclear attack on the City of Calgary, September 21, 1955.

J. E.

"Einstein," opined a lady of Rockyford
"I find, unequivocally, is not absurd
In his fine paradigm
Of space and of time,"
In response to the chime of a clock she'd heard.

"THERE ONCE WAS A MAN FROM ALBERTA..."
Limericks from Around and About Alberta

An indecisive young lady from Abee
Would answer all questions with "Maybe",
Until a young man - being kind -
Helped her make up her mind,
And now she is nursing a baby.

A hired girl from Acadia Valley
Worked as hard as any slave in a galley,
Until exhausted and sore
She collapsed on the floor,
As her boss cautioned, "Don't dilly-dally!"

Bragged a smug young fellow from Acme,
"I'm so sexy the girls all attack me:
They yank at my hair
Or kick me somewhere,
Or sometimes just haul off and smack me."

A prosperous person of Aden
Owned a swimming pool he often played in;
Not the kind you'd hold a meet in,
Or Olympians compete in,
But the plastic kind little kids wade in.

Once a carefree young fellow from Aetna
Who let the beaver he kept for a pet gnaw
At his house all day
Till his walls all gave 'way,
Said, "Do I feel one bit of regret? Nah."

A wild young housewife of Airdrie
Was as reckless as ever she dared be:
Washing coloureds with whites,
Serving sushi some nights;
She confessed, "My rebelliousness scared me."

A teacher from Alberta Beach
Said, "I find it quite easy to teach:
First of all I create
A calm classroom state,
Then I stand on my desk and I screech."

Said a farmer from near Alcomdale,
Squirting milk into his milking pail,
"There's nothing so grand
As milking by hand!"
Then was smacked by an unwelcome tail.

A young baseball pitcher of Alcurve
Threw his pitches with vigour and verve,
But displayed a great paucity
Of accuracy and velocity,
And no skill at all at making the ball curve

An unhappy young couple of Alder flats
Saw how money had caused all their spats -
Until their fortune was made
In a lucrative trade:
Do-it-yourself kits for altering cats.

A worried old woman from Alderson
Stood on the back porch and called her son,
Who was somewhere out back
With a twenty-four pack,
And wouldn't be back 'til they all were done.

Mused a hockey coach from Aldersyde,
"I'm not certain just how I'll decide
Who is playing today,
Since I bet all my pay
On a blow-out for the other side."

A disgruntled divorcee of Alexo,
In no uncertain terms, let her ex know
She would see him in court
If he missed his support;
So we now know where all of his cheques go.

Groaned a sensitive girl of Alhambra,
"I cannot stand wearing this damned bra;
It's the texture I hate -
Why can't someone create
One that's soft... say a nice Persian lamb bra?"

An amateur archeologist of Alix
Went to dig in his garden for relics,
And he found arrowheads
Beneath his flower beds
- But was hoping to dig up a Rolex.

A brilliant young man of Alliance
Once invented a kitchen appliance
To kill mice, dice and peel
And prepare a hot meal:
A true wonder of modern science!

Said a stunning ski bunny of Alpen Siding,
"I could really use help in deciding
Which clothing to wear,
And a style for my hair...
And how to keep these damned skis from sliding."

An ambitious young man of Alsask
Set himself a most difficult task.
If you're real keen on knowing
Just how well things are going,
I'm not sure - I'll wake him and ask.

A headstrong golfer from Alsike
Said, "I'll golf if I bloody well like!"
Though he saw that the lightning
On the back nine was frightening.
Who can say if he felt that bolt strike?

A spendthrift named Teresa, of Altario,
Shopped non-stop on a trip to Ontario,
But her rich rancher pa,
At the bank to withdraw,
Laughed, "How much does my little gal Terri owe?"

A rodeo rider who hailed from Amisk
Banged his back and shattered a disk;
Broke both legs and an arm,
But grinned, "Life's been a charm
When you stop to consider the risk."

Said a miss to a mean man of Andrew,
"No one here in Andrew can stand you:
You're so gross and obscene
And incredibly mean;
I'm amazed that this town hasn't banned you."

A footloose young man of Ardrossan
Left the farm for a life on the ocean
And reached officer rank
- But his leaky ship sank,
And he went down with the first mate and bos'un.

A poetic young soul of Ardenode,
Sensing imminent death penned an ode;
Then departed this life
Without kith, kin or wife,
Leaving only his pen - and an ode.

When a husky feed-handler of Anzac
Tossed about a fifty kilogram sack
He heard an old-timer brag,
"A hundredweight bag
In my day was considered a man's sack."

Said the ex-youth director of Ardmore,
"I don't quite see what I've been barred for;
I've shown, heaven knows,
Maybe twelve porno shows,
And less than two-thirds of them hard core."

A cook, who resided in Ardmore,
Said the recipes she needed lard for
Were, "My porcupine steaks
And beaver-tail cakes
- It's what I set traps in the yard for."

Many hockey fans up in Armena
Watch the games at their local arena,
But I'm told there's no way
They'll let boys and girls play,
Because girls' teams, they say, all are meaner.

A diet-crazed woman of Arrowwood
Barely eats half the food that a sparrow would,
And has slipped, twice before,
Through a crack in the floor
- something only someone very narrow could.

A reckless young driver of Ashmont
Said, "The owners of cars I have smashed want
My license revoked,
And I'm really choked:
Our society ought to be past want."

A cat-fancier once lived in Atmore
And no one, it is said, fancied cats more.
He'd say, "Cat is easily chewed
Whether broiled, baked or stewed.
After all, if not food, what's a cat for?"

A student of popular dance in Athabaska
Displayed her skill at dancing the cha-cha.
A German tourist who saw,
His voice filled with awe,
Asked, "It is for punishment you do such a task, *ja*?"

A wily, wealthy miser from Balzac
Kept all of his cash in a small sack,
Which he stored in a box
Sealed by six heavy locks,
Hidden under the floor of his small shack.

A right-wing reactionary of Banff
Was heard constantly quoting *Mein Kampf*.
Why mention this nazi?
Really? Can you not see?
There's only *Mein Kampf* rhymes with Banff.

When the wife of a farmer of Barnwell
Asked, "Whatever on earth is that darned smell?"
He was pleased to assure
Her it was just manure.
Yes, that odour she smelled was a barn smell.

Bragged a vain young lady of Barrhead,
"I possess a real movie star head,"
And no one could refute her,
Since off her computer
She'd downloaded a Hedy Lamarr head.

When a cultured young man of Bassano
Would sit down to perform at the piano,
He would, as a rule,
Fall right off his stool,
Having downed several drinks of *Cinzano*.

A bored old banker of Bashaw,
One evening while counting the cash saw
How day after day
His life slipped away;
Now he lives in a mansion in Nassau.

An ornithologist on a visit to Barons
Said, "I've come her to study your herons,"
Then drove down to the lake
And exclaimed, "Goodness sake!
These herons are really some rare ones!"

A husky young fellow from Bawlf
Decided that he'd take up golf.
In a very short while
He could drive half-a-mile
- But soon lost his balls in the rough.

A retired old lady of Beaverlodge
Each evening found reason to leave her lodge.
She would not stray too far
- Just down to the bar -
And folks at the home would believe her dodge.

A phys-ed instructor of Beaumont,
Led his class out of school for a slow jaunt,
And although nine or ten
Never came back again,
Claimed, "It's exactly what parents I know want."

A humane young fellow from Beiseker
Once pulled from the river an icy cur
Which, when kept for a pet,
Never caused him regret,
Proving once in a while some things nice occur.

Said a happy old timer from Bellview,
"From my window I look at a swell view:
It's my neighbour's wife, nude,
(And if you're into things lewd
I have photos which I'll gladly sell you.")

One winter's morning a farmer of Bentley
Arose to the snow falling gently,
But he bloody near froze
When it rose to his nose,
As the snowfall increased exponentially.

A thrifty young fellow from Bergen
Always had his eye out for a bargain,
And for a small bit of cash
Bought a huge ball of trash
- And only when the seller threw a bag in.

A sensuous lady of Berwyn
Likes warm, hairy skin next to her skin;
It is not what you think:
That skin is of mink,
Silver fox, chinchilla or ermine.

A creative young artisan from Bickerdike
Once wove, with great skill, a wicker bike.
But it sagged in the rain
And had a weak chain
- So he scrapped it and wove a much thicker bike.

There was a schoolboy from Big Coulee
Whom his teachers all claimed was unruly,
And though he did spit and swear
And grab girls by their hair,
Mom maintained they condemned him unduly.

There was an old farmer from Big Stone
Who, when ploughing one day, found a big bone,
A bone he was sure was
From a brachiosaurus,
But later found out was a pig bone.

A generous old merchant of Bindloss,
Whose employees all claimed was a kind boss,
Paid so well, it was said,
He wound up in the red,
But said, "Aw, I really don't mind loss."

A furious farmer of Black Diamond
Found his tractor's gas all had been siphoned;
But when thieves, the next day,
Towed that tractor away
His ire was considerably heightened.

When an arrogant husband of Blackie
Told his wife, "You're no more than my lackey."
She filed for divorce,
Commenting, "Of course
I could have stayed, but I'd have to be wacky."

An angry wife's husband of Blackfalds
Suffered from serious back scalds
When she threw hot tea
As he tried to flee
From that spitfire's ire in Blackfalds.

There was a young waitress of Blairmore
Whom her patrons did not really care for:
She smelled bad and was rude,
And spilled much of their food,
And they asked what in hell she was there for.

A resourceful young lady of Bodo
Tried baking, although she had no dough,
Using wallpaper paste,
And pork drippings for taste
- As you see, she was dumb as a dodo.

A *femme fatale* gal of Bon Accord,
Found her conduct was widely deplored,
But when her sins were decried,
Just shrugged and replied,
"Well, it's better than being ignored."

There was a young lady of Bondiss,
A brilliant and beautiful blond miss,
Who performed clever tricks
With lit dynamite sticks
- She's remembered by all with great fondness.

Said a clever coquette of Bonneyville,
"Only some guy whose handsome and brawny will
Ever call me his 'Honey'
- Unless he has lots of money,
Then some guy whose homely and scrawny will."

Explained an old-timer of Bowden
(That's the town he had his abode in)
"In July it's nice here,
But the rest of the year
I can't get out 'cause I'm snowed in."

A nostalgic old Scot of Bow Island
Said, "Ma' heart is in the Highland;
Ma' bladder in Trieste,
Both kidneys in Brest,
And ma' bowels, I believe, are in Thailand."

Yawned an indolent farmer of Boyle,
With an avowed aversion to toil,
"I know nothing less thrilling
Or more unfulfilling
Than unwillingly tilling the soil."

There once was a man from Bragg Creek
Who was known as a bit of a geek;
He'd seek clothing stores where
Female mannequins were bare,
Then would furtively go sneak a peek.

An unpleasant old person of Breynat
Forever found things to complain at,
But his wife shrugged and said,
Inside of his head
Was a void where there should be a brain at.

A man with a poultry farm in Breton
Who, one damp, rainy night, tried to let in
His cold, soaking flock
Lost the key to the lock,
So just stood there, as mad as a wet hen.

A rather dim fellow from Brocket,
Who stuck a fork in an empty light socket,
Cried, "Hey, this is alright!
I feel kind of bright!"
- Then scientifically constructed a rocket.

Said a forthright young lady of Brooks,
"I admit I have never read books;
But since fate has been kind,
Both before and behind,
I shall simply get by on my looks."

A disappointed young fellow of Brosseau,
Distressed by a dinner-date no show,
Later heard that girl say,
"What? Show up? No way!
Last time *I* had to pay - It's a no-go!"

An ardent bird hunter from Bruce
Every fall, without fail, hunted goose.
He did not use a gun,
But found it more fun
Just to lasso a goose with a noose.

Griped an angry young student of Bruce,
"My schoolmates are really obtuse;
I was shoved in a slough
Where I lost my left shoe:
I'm a victim of '*so-shallow*' abuse.'"

There once was a poet of Bruderheim,
And no one has since written a lewder rhyme:
It told of a cow,
Two mules and a plow...
- You can see 'way back then was a ruder time.

An unmotivated teacher of Buffalo
Said, "Sure, I could teach kids this stuff I know,
But I fear some small brain
Might collapse from the strain:
Who would wish to see any child suffer so?"

A worried young woman of Burmis
Felt a pain in her epidermis,
And took to her bed
'Til a wise doctor said,
"I've discovered the cause - it's a burr, Miss."

The boys' hockey team up in Cadomin
Last Tuesday night finally had a win.
As a result of deep snow
The other team was 'no show',
But, really, it wasn't so bad a win.

Said a young cowboy-artist of Calgary
"If only I could make my sweet gal agree
To mount a horse and then pose
Without wearin' no clothes,
I could paint a picture that would sell in a gallery."

A sentimental soul of Calmar
Kept his gallstones preserved in a bell jar
Which he placed on display
Whenever folks came to stay
In his tasteful little home in Calmar.

Screamed a panicky woman from Camrose,
They'd be drowned if the water in the dam rose,
Though her friends tried in vain
To clearly explain
There was no damn dam near to Camrose.

There once was a widow of Canmore,
And nobody wanted a man more:
He could shovel her snow
And provide her with dough
… But that's *all* she wanted a man for

Advised a wise father from Cardston,
"If you're sure to be always on guard, son,
Against come-hither smiles
And feminine wiles,
Your life will be empty and hard, son."

A risqué young lady of Caroline
Would frequently tread a quite narrow line,
And would freely confess,
"My very tight dress
Does reveal - as you see - my whole panty-line."

A man who lived in Carrot Creek
Once taught his pet parrot to speak:
It gave memorable orations
At the United Nations
In Swahili, Early Hebrew and Greek.

A compulsive old liar from Carseland
Said, “I know all them big TV stars, and
Great statesmen await
For advice at my gate
… And out back’s where them creatures from Mars
land.”

Boasted a bubbling booster of Carstairs,
“No other towns’ fairs are like our fairs:
We have chickens and ducks
And pickup trucks
- And no mayor’s overalls are like our mayor’s”

A would-be musician of Carvel
Believed he could play his guitar well,
But the sound of his play
Made the cat run away
And his poor old dog whimper and grovel.

A sweet old lady from Carway
Went off on a visit to Norway
When asked, “Is it near?”
Replied, “Oh, no, My Dear,
That damn place is terribly far away.”

A creative inventor of Castor
Built a houseboat entirely of plaster,
Then proceeded to take
His friends out on the lake,
Thus creating a minor disaster.

A tautological teacher of Cayley
Warned students not wishing to fail he
Expected each to complete
A complete study sheet
Every day… once a day… each day… daily.

There was an old plumber of Cental
With assets - although none was mental -
Who owned a huge septic tank
That gurgled and stank,
And which he offered to folks as a rental.

A daring young seamstress of Cereal
Sewed a gown out of see-through material,
And though the women of town
Turned away with a frown.
All the boys found that gown quite etherial.

Said a sensitive soul Cessford,
"Our town's name is not really the best word,
So I've sought to arrange
To author a change
So we can become '*Crappy-Messford*'."

An esoteric homemaker from Champion
Made a stew for her family from *rampion,*
A plant so obscure
She had to assure
Them this food was quite okay to chomp on.

A willful young child of Cheadle
Said, "I get what I want when I wheedle,
Cajole, whine or carp,
Or whimper or harp,
Or - failing all else - simply needle."

A delusional prospector of Cherhill
Said, "Folks think that there's only a bare hill."
Then he'd point to a mound
About twelve feet around:
"There's a fortune in gold in that there hill."

A proud pork producer of Chauvin
Showed some feminist tourists, who drove in,
A male chauvinist pig,
Mean, ugly and big:
A he-devil whose vile feet were cloven.

Though a busty babe of Chestermere Lake
Stretched her swimsuit with each breathe she'd take,
It was found she'd been adding
Huge wads of thick padding
- Thus revealing her chest a mere fake.

A romantic young miss of Chinook
Claimed, "My heart is a wide-open book!"
But what guy would marry
A lending library?
For that was the role that she took.

Said a man living in Chinook Valley
Who took part in an anarchist rally,
"I'd join their club in a minute
But there's nobody in it…
They must really not want to get pally."

Said a carefree old drifter of Claresholm,
"Wherever I go anywhere's home.
Why, I've slept in a shed
And a shack with no bed…
…And once, I recall, Old John Ware's home."

A centenarian who lived in Cline River
And drove about in a Model T flivver,
Said, "I don't need to be told
We are both very old
And we cough, shudder, sputter and quiver."

A clever bee keeper of Clive
Does not keep any bees in a hive.
"No, I keep them, instead,
In the springs of my bed
- And what sweet, sweet dreams I derive!"

An enterprising housewife of Cluny
Sold her husband one day for a loonie,
Remarking, "I feel
Got the best of that deal:
He was lazy… and ugly… and puny."

A confirmed old tippler of Coaldale
Voiced a personal preference for old ale
… and new ale… and stale ale
… and dark ale… and pale ale
… and for piping hot, tepid and cold ale.

Said a fatherly rancher of Cochrane,
"I believe it is time for a talk, Son,
About the birds and the bees,
And how loud one should sneeze…
You do know that's what's making our stock run?"

Said a hunter who lived in Cold Lake,
And shot his best friend by mistake,
"I admit that I drilled him,
But I winged him, not killed him,
So c'mon, man - gimme a break!"

A motivational speaker, while in Coleman,
Proclaimed he would develop the whole man;
But a one-legged man
Yelled, "I don't think you can!"
Now, wasn't that fellow a drole man?

A cowboy who lived in Compeer
Once decided he'd wrestle a steer,
But that steer knew some tricks
- Won four falls of six -
(And the prize - a half-dozen of beer)

A misguided young lady of Consort
Hung about with a crowd of the wrong sort;
Still, no one could get her
To seek something better
Since her character wasn't the strong sort.

A prominent politician of Coronation
Had an illness causing great consternation
Until a specialist came
- A physician of fame -
And diagnosed it extreme constipation.

A smuggler who live down in Coutts
Crossed the border by numerous routes,
And though American scouts
Claimed, "We know all his routes."
They did nothing - were they in cahoots?

"Begone!" Screeched an irate wife of Cowley,
"You're vile, and you've acted most foully!"
To which her husband replied,
"Dear, I'll just step outside,
And come back when you're feeling less owly."

A curious girl of Craigmyle
Continually wore a vague smile.
Did something confuse her?
... Or maybe amuse her?
... Or was that just simply her style?

An idle young lady of Cremona
Lounged all day in her flimsy Kimono,
And did so until
She contracted a chill
And subsequently died of pneumonia.

An assertive young fellow of Crossfield
Flat-out insisted his boss yield
When he argued one day
For an increase in pay
- After all, how much clout does a boss yield?

A wise-ass from Crows Nest Pass
Skied nude and - of course - froze his ass,
Then in order to thaw it
- Claimed a witness who saw it-
He farted and ignited the gas.

Asked a classical scholar of Cynthia,
"I wonder, would a nice marble plinth be a
A base that would do
For our fast food drive-thru?
I believe one may be found in Corinthia."

An aspiring young actress of Czar
Said, "I hope to one day be a cstar;
But, alas, her car crashed
And the windshield was smashed,
And she's marred by a hideous cscar.

An eccentric old trapper of Dapp
Claimed he'd once caught Bigfoot in a trap,
But all who heard would agree
The old boy must be
One hundred percent full of crap.

A young country singer from Daysland
Aspired to one day sing at Graceland,
But her voice was so flat
It was obvious that
She'd be consigned to some musical wasteland.

Out dining, a fine lady of Del Bonita
Asked the waiter "Please bring me a pita."
It was quickly prepared,
But she no longer cared,
Having now downed her sixth margarita.

A curious tourist of Delburne
Took an overnight flight clear to Melbourne,
And found it a wonder
When he was Down-Under
That Melbourne was quite unlike Delburne.

Said a laid-back dude living in Delia,
Who face was one giant camellia,
"Folks notice it a lot;
It's a tattoo I got:
Memorabilia of my psychedelia."

There was a young lady from Demmit
Who would buy a new dress and then hem it:
She would measure and cut
'Til that hem reached her butt.
(Still, no guy in Demmit would condemn it.)

A sweet-talking farm boy of Derwent
Complimented his sweetie on her scent,
An exotic perfume
Which infused all the room.
"It sure smells lots better than manure scent."

A tipsy old dipso of Devon
Would stagger home about half-past eleven.
Then he ran out of luck
And was struck by a truck
- Let us pray he resides now in heaven.

A frustrated mother of Didsbury
Wondered, what was it made her kids scurry
When supper was served?
It was what she deserved,
Since she constantly fed those kids curry.

A reeve of the town of Donalda
Summoned all of his council and called a
Meeting to say
They were meeting next day,
-A redundancy for Donalda in Donalda.

There was a strange lady of Donnely
Whose life seemed to be an anomaly:
Though she seemed quite the prude,
She would dance in the nude
In her church when the priest gave his homily.

An extremely ill woman of Drayton Valley
Almost miraculously started to rally,
As her husband, looking glum,
Crumpled the paper with the sum
Of her insurance, of which he'd just done a tally.

A resourceful young girl of Drumheller
Worked each day in the bank as a teller,
And each evening would stash
Large bundles of cash
In a hole which she'd dug in her cellar.

A faith healer, on a visit to Duchess,
Told a sceptical girl, "My touch is
The cure that you hope for."
Then proceeded to grope for
Her thighs… Now he hobbles on crutches.

A solemn old doctor of Dunsmore
Sighed, "This man, I'm afraid, is done for;
That scratch on his scalp
Means he's far beyond help."
Don't you think he perhaps could have done more?

A passionate damsel of Dunsmore
Whispered sweetly and softly, "Just one more."
Not expressing a wish
For a sweet, tender kiss,
But one more of those beers she had come for.

Said a twisted old teacher of Eckville,
"Any person who bothers to check will
Find I teach a series
Of paranoid theories -
'Cause if I don't teach them, who the heck will?"

A wily old widower of Edson
Turned to his sole offspring and said, "Son,
If we each had a wife
They could feed us for life...
So let us both go and get wed, Son."

A young girl who lived in Elk Point
Joined her friends in smoking a joint,
And all day held some meat
In thick smoke and low heat
- Because that's how you smoke a joint in Elk Point.

A devious woman of Elkwater
Eluded all the mounties who sought her.
They were hot on her tail,
(She forged phoney junk mail)
And - thank heavens - those cops finally caught her.

A hefty young fellow from Edmonton
Proved incredibly agile at badminton;
Nor was he dismayed
When asked what he weighed:
"With the weight of the birdie," he said, "One ton."

When an elegant girl of Elkwater
Rejected a young man who sought her,
He said, with a smile,
"I'll just wait for awhile
Then come back and I'll marry her daughter."

A very vain lady of Empress,
On a trip to the cleaners, had them press
A skirt hemmed so high
It bared half of her thigh,
For she fancied herself quite a temptress.

A gorgeous young girl of Enchant
Causes boys there to sigh and to pant;
Even in her most drab dress
She remains an enchantress.
- Wise men try to explain this, yet can't.

An enterprising farmer of Entwhistle
Felt his fortune could be made growing sisal.
It all came to a stop
When his crop was a flop
And his fields yielded nothing but thistle.

A junoesque maiden of Esther
Found that men always wanted to test her,
In hopes they could beat
Her at some physical feat,
Yet not one of them ever could best her.

Said a very wise parent of Etzicom,
"If our weird daughter Betsy ever gets a bomb
We must try to disarm her,
And in no way should harm her,
- Though we first must get our little Betsy calm."

A physician who serves Eureka River
Told a patient all the facts he could give her:
"Your lungs seem okay,
And your heart pumps away
- I'd say liquor explains your weak liver."

An observant young lady from Exshaw
Spied the King of Iran in a rickshaw,
And cried out in dismay,
"When you travel this way
Aren't you frightened of breaking your neck, Shah?"

A frugal young fellow from Fahler
Tipped an eighty-buck meal with a dollar,
And later, of course,
Felt pangs of remorse
Because he hadn't had anything smaller.

An immodest old matron from Fairview
Offered those in the street a rare view
When she strolled around town
In a cellophane gown...
A sight most, to be sure, would not care to view.

There was an old fellow of Faust
Whom his wife was unable to roust,
And fearing him dead
Called the doctor, who said,
"The old boy's just thoroughly soused."

A dog owner living in Fawcett
Would pick up a stick and then toss it,
But feel totally wretched
When the dog failed to fetch it
- That pooch would not let anyone boss it.

Sighed a disenchanted lady of Finnegen,
"I am so sick and tired of these skinny men;
I go hunt for a stud
And bag some scrawny dud:
In love's lottery shall I never win again?"

A young hockey forward from Foremost
Who hammered his head on a goalpost
Chuckled, "Time and again
I rattle my brain,
But that seems to be just when I score most."

A compulsive young man of Forestburg
Became overcome with a 'florist urge',
And spent many happy hours
In his shop full of flowers:
It certainly wasn't his worst urge.

A young girl from Fort Chipeweyan
Became pen pals with a distant Hawaiian
Who sent her (spoiler alert!)
A real colourful shirt
And a grass skirt she has yet to try on.

A rancher from down 'round Fort Macleod
Found most city folks trendy and loud,
So he'd saddle his horse
And set off on some course
Which led him far from the fadding crowd.

A lady living in Fort McMurray
Had a husband who caused her some worry;
At times she could swear
He resembled a bear:
He was huge, had big paws, and was furry.

A romantic young swain of Fox Creek
Placed a kiss on a young maiden's cheek,
But she recoiled in disgust,
Saying, "Really, you must
Quit chewing on garlic - you reek!"

An ostrich producer of Fort Saskatchewan
Said, "I'll just step outside and I'll catch you one.
He came back forlorn,
His clothing all torn,
Saying, "I'll just get an egg and I'll hatch you one.

An optimist who dwelt at Frog Lake
Backed straight into that lake by mistake,
But as he watched his car sink,
Cried, "It's so great to think
I got out. Wow! This is one lucky break!"

A paranoid person of Gem
Said, "I'm not really one to condemn,
But I cannot quite see
Why it's them against me
When it ought to be me against them.

At the fair, a fair maiden of Gibbons
Was awarded a number of ribbons.
It was not cakes or pies
Which had earned her each prize,
But her exhibits for the young guys of Gibbons.

A romantic young maiden of Girouxville
Whose existence provided her zero thrill,
Said, "I really don't care,
I shall never despair,
For I know someday my shining hero will."

A practical lady of Gleichen
Had a pan which she stored her dog's leash in,
For she claimed that the fleas
Helped flavour the cheese
When she used that same pan to bake quiche in.

A sorry young man from Grande Cache
Was addicted to both coke and hash:
He just could not stop
Guzzling down pop,
And that corned beef ate up all his cash.

A merchant who lived in Grand Centre
Staged a raffle all the townsfolk could enter.
The prize was a shoe.
- He didn't have two -
And he, himself, was the formal presenter.

A delusional man of Grand Prairie
Was convinced he was a canary,
And was terrified that
He'd be caught by the cat
(Which we all must admit would be scary.)

A self-proclaimed psychic of Grassy Lake
Could - according to claims he would make -
Foretell future events
With his potent sixth sense
- But was, in fact, a foolish, fatuous fake.

An industrious lady of Granum
Said, "I trap lots of gophers and can 'em
- I tan their hides, too -
And with my grasshopper stew
It brings in several hundred per annum."

A venerable old geezer of Grimshaw
Would practice the odd craft of Scrimshaw
And engrave, with detail,
The huge tooth of whale
- Which was not readily come by in Grimshaw.

A scientific-minded man of Grouard Mission
Likes to dabble in nuclear fission,
But a minor mistake
Could spell the end of Gift Lake
As well as Grourd, Atikameg - and Grourd Mission.

The little French hamlet of Guy
Has a curious name - as you'll see -
For although you and I
Might pronounce it as "Guy",
Every francophone guy knows it's "Guy".

A lazy young loafer of Halkirk
Had a major aversion to all work;
Though he played pool all day
And won money that way,
It was hardly a thing you could call 'work'.

A charming young dancer from Hardisty
Was known far and wide for her modesty,
And all through each show
Would blush head-to-toe
In the strip joint where she practiced her artistry.

For his lunch, a *grand gourmet* of Hanna
Hankered after a fresh-picked banana,
So flew off to Brazil,
Where his boat chanced to spill,
Giving lunch to a school of piranha.

An anxious old timer from Hairy Hill
Said, "I've lived my whole life on this very hill.
But it's all up and down,
Not one flat piece of ground,
And at my age I find it a scary hill."

There was a young lady from Hayter
Who could not find a boy who would date her;
Perhaps it was that
She chewed snoose and spat,
But for some reason guys seemed to hate her.

A free spirit, who lived in High Level,
One cold winter's night went to revel,
But he froze both his nose
And all ten of his toes.
(Which, you know, really hurts like the devil!)

A self-assured girl of High Prairie
Said, "I insist that the man I marry
Will see things my way
And do just as I say."
- But none did; they were all much too wary.

A dissolute old man of High River,
Who confessed he had been a high-liver,
Grumbled, "What did I get?
A mountain of debt
And a passel of spots on my liver."

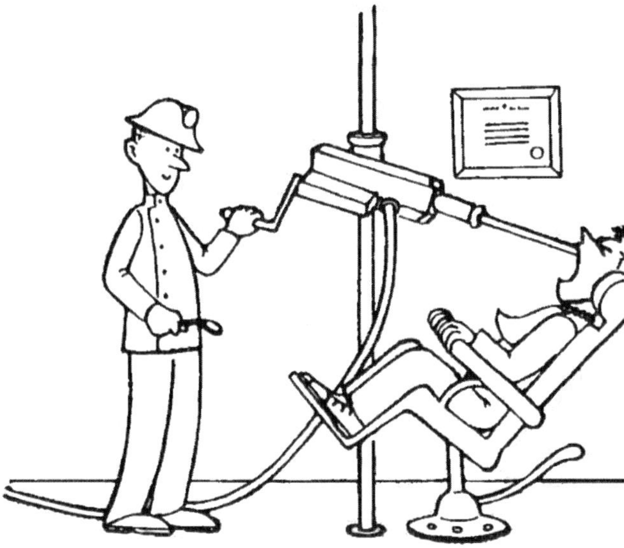

A dentist from the coal town of Hillcrest
Said, "Oral prevention is still best,
But if it comes down to drilling
When a tooth needs a filling,
I still find my pneumatic drill best."

An Aussie tourist, out hunting near Hilda,
Took aim with his rifle and killed a
Moose and a goose
And a cow that was loose,
And wounded poor waltzing Matilda.

There was a young boy of Hines Creek
Who loved to go play hide-and-seek,
Until he hid in a truck
And the door became stuck,
- And he was stuck in that truck for a week.

A voluptuous lady of Hinton
Pulled a sweater the colour of mint on,
And the gallants of town
Volunteered to brush down
Any section that sweater got lint on.

There was a shy maiden of Holden
Whom a couple of drinks would embolden;
But then a couple more
Left her flat on the floor
- For which everyone was beholden.

An auto body repairman of Hondo
Rebuilt a Honda with homemade Bondo,
But he felt bitter pain:
It dissolved in the rain
- Consequently generating him no dough.

A balmy old booze-hound from Hughenden
Would stroll up to a barman he knew and then
Ask, "Good Sir, do you think
You might stand me a drink?"
As the barman groaned, "Jeez… not you again!"

An aspiring country musician of Hussar
Lacked the wherewithal to buy a guitar,
But owned a small ukulele
Which he practiced on daily.
(His career did not go very far.)

A prosperous person of Hylo
Is the wealthiest guy that I know.
He owns cannabis shops
On high mountain tops;
His motto? "Sell high - buy low."

A gluttonous lady of Hythe
With regards to her diet seemed blithe:
"Though I eat like a pig
I never grow big,
But remain ever svelte, lean and lithe."

Some athletic young ladies of Indus
Said "Running a race does not wind us,
Nor biking all day,
Nor the games we all play…
Carrying plywood against a strong wind does."

A dairyman from out around Innisfail
Once discovered a gopher drowned in his pail.
He glanced slyly about,
Pulled the dead gopher out,
Then wrung out the milk he found in its tail.

A devout old woman of Inisfree
Said, "I so often dream of a time to be
When someone takes my hand
To lead me to that land
Where the beer's always cold and the gin is free."

There once was a lady from Irma
Named Irma, who travelled to Burma;
And then, very soon,
Came a card from Rangoon:
It was from Irma from Irma from Burma.

When a foreword young lady of Jasper
Invited a young man to grasp her,
He complied with such zest
Her breasts were compressed,
And she requested he kindly unclasp her.

An brilliant young poet of Jenner
Was renowned for being the penner
Of classical odes
And poems about toads,
And dirges, to be sung by a tenor.

A stubborn old man of Kathleen
Is convinced - and always has been -
A toothbrush and toothpaste
Are a fanciful waste;
- Hence the reason his teeth are all green.

Bragged a bow hunter up in Keg River,
"Killin' grizzlies - that's all that I live for!"
Searchers found his red hat
All chewed up - only that
And a tiny, wee piece of his quiver.

A myopic old hunter of Killam
Claimed, "I was a good shot, and I still am;
I'm not good at a distance
But with patient persistence
Birds perch on my gun and I drill 'em."

Chirped an elderly songstress of Kitskoty,
"Now my voice is engaging and throaty,
And has matured like fine wine."
But those who heard were inclined
To say she sounded like a dying Coyote.

An old trapper from near Lac La Biche
Strolled through town with a bear on a leash.
Later asked if aware
His pet was a bear,
Mumbled, "Nope... I smoked too much hashish."

A singular lad of Lacombe
Had a head which resembled a dome,
And though thought to contain
A magnificent brain,
It was "lights out and nobody home".

A young teacher who lived in La Glace
Tattooed her own face on her ass,
But the superintendent
Snapped, "That's it! Let's end it!"
So now that young lass has no class.

Said a buxom young belle of Lake Louise,
"Getting boyfriends is really a breeze!
I just keep a sharp eye
'Til some cool guy comes by
Then I tackle him right at the knees!"

A maladroit curate of Lamont
Who dropped his watch in the baptismal font
Says his time is now reckoned
By "Every blessed second."
What more could a pious priest want?

An obnoxious young fellow of Langdon
Had a drum he incessantly banged on,
And his neighbours, it's true,
Still can - and still do -
Show the tree in his yard he was hanged on.

A roughneck who worked near Leduc
Swilled down beer 'til it caused him to puke,
But he said, with a smile,
"I can do this with style,"
Then discretely threw up in his toque.

"You pronounce," said a man of Legal,
"The name of our village *trés mal,*
But since myself I speak singularly
Most unbilingularly,
A moi, tout ça c'est égal."

A concerned, irate mother of Legerton
Is miffed local police have accused her son
Of swiping lollipops and gumdrops,
Jellybeans and soda pops,
And a car from the bar on the edge of town.

A dentist who resided in Lethbridge
Installed his young daughter Beth's bridge:
She'd ignored his appeals
To brush after meals
And her teeth had fallen out in Lethbridge.

"When we moved in," said a lady of Linden,
"This house was as neat as a new pin,
But wouldn't you know,
Six kids in a row
Have turned it into a regular pigpen."

An agreeable young lad of Little Smoky,
Responded to all requests, "Okey-dokey,"
Then sold a friend's pills
And passed counterfeit bills,
- So now he's confined to the pokey.

A retiring young maid of Lloydminster
Was resigned to the life of a spinster
'Til a young man who met her
Claimed there was something better,
And, by George! he completely convinced her!

An alarmed old logger of Lodgepole
Saw his pickup, a rusty old Dodge, roll
Downhill to a lake
(He had not set his brake)
Onto the ice, and down through a large hole.

An unfortunate fellow of Lomond
Nearly choked when he swallowed an almond,
Then was stung by a bee,
Fell and fractured his knee…
Could it be that his life was ill-omened?

A rancher who lived west of Longview
Was known to hold many a strong view,
Among which, the chief
Was *one shouldn't eat beef.*
Which seemed, to his neighbours, the wrong view.

When a card-sharp, whose home was in Lundbreck,
For a high-stakes game doctored up one deck,
The success of his play
Quickly gave him away.
... They say he lies buried beneath his sun deck.

Crowed a weight-conscious maid of Magrath,
"I'm so slender - just thin as a lath."
But one night must have surely
Pulled the plug prematurely
And was sucked down the drain of her bath.

There once was a lady of Mallaig
Who discovered a nest with a small egg;
Once she'd cracked it and beaten it
And fried up and eaten it
Said, "There was barely enough there to call egg."

Enjoined a preacher from Ma-Me-O Beach,
"No object lies beyond mankind's reach,..."
As he shoplifted booze
And a new pair of shoes,
"...And I am practicing that which I preach."

Groaned a sickly young fellow of Mannville,
Whose bowels were as hard as an anvil,
"Is there nothing can cure
This great pain I endure?"
The answer, of course, would be, "Bran will."

An unhappy young maid of Manyberries
Says she'll move far away if she marries.
Then she'll tremble and cry,
"I've been living a lie:
This darned place does not have any berries."

A distraught young man of Marlboro
Staggered out of the Income tax bureau.
"They took my wallet and phone
And every last dime I own
- But I really do find them most thorough."

A famed country musician from Marwayne,
Found fakin' all his guitar playin',
Was dragged from the stage
By his fans, in a rage,
And he knew he was seein' his star wane.

Said an aging egotist of Mayerthorpe,
"Yeah, I've noticed my outer layer warp
As the years have rolled by,
But no one can deny
I'm still the best looking guy in Mayerthorpe."

A clever young man of McClennan
Built a house using mortise and tenon
- A joint-forming technique,
Light, strong and unique -
Saying, "I enjoy a nice joint now and then.".

A pharmacist of Medicine Hat
Once concocted some medicine that
Was so crystalline clear
It would quite disappear,
And would moan, “Where’s my medicine at?”

There was a young lady of Medley
Who drank bottles of mineral water steadily,
But did not suspect
Concretions might collect
In her innards - nor that they’d be deadly.

There was an old farmer of Metiskow
Who, for reasons unknown, would let his cow
Trample his potatoes,
And his corn and tomatoes
- And it appears to be trampling his lettuce now.

Mused a beef-loving gourmet of Millet
As he fried up a fish in a skillet,
“If I had my way
This would be a filet,
But I guess I’ll make do with a fillet.”

A freaky old farmer of Milo
Kept six kids and a pig in his silo
- As well as his wife.
Who calls this a life?
Really, nobody I know.

In the bar a young fellow of Morinville
Kept drinking more and more until
He had blown all his pay.
Who behaves in this way?
A wise person won't, but a moron will.

A brave pioneer woman of Monitor
Faced hardships poets write sonnets for:
They tell how mice ate her hay,
Or how her cow ran away,
Or that one windy day her puffy bonnet tore.

A mailman from down in Milk River
Was lean - Just as thin as a sliver;
So gaunt you might doubt
He could pack mail about
- But gals claimed he could really deliver.

Cautioned a virtuous maiden of Mirror
To her boyfriend, "Don't come any nearer."
But when he got there
She appeared not to care,
Delighted he'd seemed not to hear her.

Said a hopeful young man of Mundare,
On whose head there remained but one hair,
"Though my hair-loss seems chronic,
With the help of this tonic
I could salvage the one hair that's there."

Said an underground trader from Myrnam,
"It ain't nobody's business what I earn, man.
Sure, I buy and I sell
And, yeah, do real well
- But for sure won't tell no tax return man."

An adventurous man of Namaka
Went to Aukland and brought back a
Beautiful Maori,
- His new wife - and her dowry;
Now they happily do the *haka* in Namaka.

A kindly old lady of Nanton
Had a stand which she kept a large plant on,
But the police came one day
And took all three away
- So the situation took a new slant on.

Once a handsome young man from Neerlandia
Met a lovely young lady from Scandia,
Then he searched up and down
To locate that small town
- The home of that darling girl, Andrea.

There was a young man of New Briden,
And the one thing he truly took pride in
Was his ten-ton Chevrolet
- bought for his wedding day -
For transporting hogs and his bride in.

Said a brilliant young author of New Brook,
"I am considering writing a new book;
I shall fill up the pages
With a tale for the ages:
Instructions for delicious dishes you cook."

Because an amateur actor of Nisku
Would get to his line and then miscue,
His cohorts ran a string
From his shorts to one wing,
Saying, "Next time he won't miss on his cue."

An ill-mannered old man of New Norway
Would pee from his farmhouse doorway.
When questioned as to why,
He'd zip up his fly and reply,
"I'll do it my way; you do it your way."

An artful old scamp of New Sarepta,
- Although no one for sure knew - kept a
Still beneath his porch
Where he made homemade hooch
- Of course, all of his neighbours suspected.

Vowed a gossipy girl from Nobleford,
"It's a secret and I'll never tell a word!"
Then off she would go
To let all the world know
Every single word she had just heard.

A man who had grown up in No Jack,
Now wealthy, decided he'd go back.
He donned fine new attire,
But his car blew a tire
And - wouldn't you know? - he had no jack.

An out-of-work miner from Nordeg
Told his wife he really abhorred egg
In his Sunday brunch,
But she had a hunch
It was simply they couldn't afford egg.

A nerdy young fellow from Okotoks
Was often the butt of local jokes
Until he stopped being nice
And with a nuclear device
Half-frightened to death all the local folks.

A delicate damsel of Olds
Was afflicted with coughs and with colds,
And would sneeze without stop
Until moist 'round the top,
And her dress was discoloured with molds.

A matronly lady of Oyen
Saw herself as society's doyenne,
And wallpapered the shed
Where the piglets were fed
- The mark of a true social lion.

An adventuresome fellow of Onoway
Said, "Good-bye, Onoway, I'm on my way."
Those asking around
Where might he be found
Were told, "Can't rightly say; he's gone away."

A shapely young shopper of Orion
Said, "There's swimwear here I'd like to try on.
Do you think you could see me
In a mini bikini?"
Now, there's someone you might keep your eye on.

A gentleman of Paradise Valley
Once engaged a high-priced valet
To polish his boots,
Dig up dandelion roots,
And lead his pigs on parade down the alley.

A patriotic lad of Patricia
Marched off to join the militia,
Never guessing, of course,
He'd be sent with a force
To guard garbage dumps in far-off Silesia.

An old man with a young wife in Peace River,
When asked what bequest he might give her -
What he'd leave his young wife
Upon departing this life -
Answered, "Nothin' - I plan to outlive her."

Said a lady at a ball game in Peers,
"In Peers no one gets cheers or jeers;
As you can tell by our name,
We're all treated the same;
Here in Peers we are all peers, my Dears."

A philosopher-farmer of Penhold
Questioned many beliefs that men hold:
He asked, "What lights the stars?"
"Is there life upon Mars?"
And, "How many pigs should a pen hold?"

An old shoemaker from Picture Butte
Told a rancher, "I've mended your boot."
- But in place of the heel
He'd installed a small wheel,
Thus inciting a bitter dispute.

A would-be young golfer of Pivot,
Known for tearing up many a divot,
Claimed, when he spoke
Of technique and of stroke,
"I just close both eyes and I *give it*."

A *belle femme who* lived up in Plamondon,
Greeted each day with a *belle chanson,*
And since all there could see
Her *grande joie de vie,*
Why, they just joined right in and sang along.

Said a sage old rancher from Pollockville,
"Go out into your field and stand stock-still;
Them curious cows
Will approach as they browse
- At least I'm hoping a few of *my* lost stock will."

A coffee connoisseur of Ponoka
Voiced preference for *café mocha,*
Which he drank to excess
Until caffein-induced stress
Sent him into paroxysms of the polka.

Bragged a restauranteur of Provost,
"A bad host is better than no host."
Then he'd break wind, or curse,
Or do something much worse,
So at present he occupies no post.

A modest miss, a sweet girl of Pincher Creek,
Told her beau that he could pinch her cheek,
But she dealt him a blow
When that rascal went low
- Could she know that he would pinch her *cheek*?

At an auction an old rancher of Priddis
Said, "I don't really care what the bid is;
Once I've sold my last steer
I'll start my new career
As a fashion designer's apprentice."

There is an old cowboy from Queenstown
Who saunters 'round town with his jeans down
To where they show some
Of the crack in his bum
- And everyone gasps when he leans down.

At a party, when a young maid of Raymond
Heard a guest say his flowers were 'stamened'
She collapsed in a faint,
For, although it sounds quaint,
They don't speak of sex down in Raymond.

A profound young preacher of Redcliff
Warned, "Everyone in this church would be dead if
The sun ceased to burn,"
Then sensing concern,
Added, "You must remember I said 'if'."

A worried old woman of Red Deer
Once turned to her husband and said, "Dear,
You've sat days in that chair
With a glazed, empty stare,
And I fear that perhaps you are dead, Dear."

An adventuresome father of Redwater
Climbed a lookout with his over-fed daughter.
When she leaned on a railing
She crashed through the paling
- Lucky for that daughter, dad caught her.

Years ago a dull dimwit of Rimby
Evoked the question, "Can someone this dim be
Of use - or become
Much more than a bum?"
He now heads our Provincial Assembly.

A trucker living in Rochfort Bridge
Was once hired to deliver a fridge,
Which he found he must wrestle
Over a half-mile of trestle.
Did it tire him? Well... maybe a smidge.

A taxidermist who served Rocky Mountain House
Worked hours in vain just to mount a grouse;
When success came at last
His joy quickly passed:
His next client's wish was to mount a mouse.

A crafty young rascal of Rolling Hills
Was renowned for his masterful trolling skills.
He would never upset
Anyone on ‘the net’,
But caught fish in small nets by their gills.

A volunteer fireman from Rosiland
Seized hold of his firehose nozzle and
Attempted to soak
His truck - shrouded in smoke -
The result of a drill… mmm… not so well-planned.

A little girl living in Rumsy
Called out to her horrified Mumsy,
“I’ve cut off all my hair;
Now my head is quite bare…
But I really do think it becomes me!”

Said a righteous old farmer from Rycroft
Who stored his hay away up in a high loft,
“When them couples from town
Get to foolin’ around
They dang well better stay out of my loft!”

The boys' hockey coach up in Rolly View
Tried a goal-tending change which was wholly new:
A pretty girl donned the pads,
While some curious dads
Asked, how well would this new comely goalie do?

A full-figured maiden of Ryley
Would curtsy, and then smile shyly,
When the owner would announce her
As the resident bouncer
At his bar, where she tossed out drunks nightly.

A jealous young husband from St. Albert,
Incensed at seeing his wife and best pal flirt,
Sent the two of them packing,
Though he found it heart-wracking,
For the loss of a really good pal hurt.

When a charming young girl of St. Paul
Strolled downtown dressed in a qt. shawl,
A policeman explained
Why she'd been detained;
"Sure, a girl can wear a shawl - but that at. All."

There was a young man of Sangudo
Who proved most proficient at Judo,
But the lady he wed
-A pole dancer- said,
"I know lots more moves than what you do."

Mused an elderly woman of Saunders,
Who sits alone by her window and ponders
Why her husband disappears
- And sometimes for years -
"I guess the old bugger just wanders."

There is a young lady of Scandia
- A charming young maid name of Andrea -
And I've heard, so it's said,
She's now shares her bed
With a handsome young man from Neerlandia

Once a questionable gentleman of Schuler
Gave his girl a ring he'd 'bought from a jeweller'.
She examined that ring,
Then yelled, "This crappy thing
Is a fake!" - See? His scam didn't fool her.

A disillusioned young fellow from Sexsmith
Who once used his phone to talk sex with,
Said, "Instead of a thrill
I just got a big bill;
So I've heard quite enough of this 'sex myth'.

A sadistic little brat of Sherwood Park
Fed the canary to the cat for a lark,
But just fates would decree
That on a trip to the sea
He'd be eaten up whole by a shark.

An excited old fellow of Sedgewick
Shouted, "Maude, come look by the hedge, quick!
Them aliens are back
And they've put George in a sack,
And I think it's an attack upon Sedgewick!"

Some volunteer firemen of Sibbald
Sat in their fire truck and quibbled
- Silhouetted by flame-
As to who was to blame
For the reason their hose only dribbled.

A refined young lady of Skiff,
Who awoke one day feeling stiff,
Took a tumbler of gin,
Threw some Tylenol in,
And smiled, "I'll feel fine in a jiff."

A vegetarian from up in Slave Lake
Said, "Sometimes I *do* crave a steak,
But then all I do
Is chew on a shoe
Which I garnish with dry Shake 'n Bake."

A brilliant inventor from Smith
Amazed everyone, coming up with
Electrified shorts
For our cold winter sports
- Thus becoming a cultural myth.

The organizer of a stag at Smoky Lake
Arranged for a nude girl to pop from a cake
He had the shock of his life:
That 'girl' was his wife
... But she gave him a cut of the take.

A lovely young lady from Speddin
Chose the gown she wished to be wed in,
But a bridesmaid would say
- In a most catty way -
"There's one dress I would not be caught dead in."

A preacher who preached in Spirit River
Had a spirited sermon he'd deliver
In which he would yell
Of damnation and Hell
As parishioners hollered out "Give 'er!"

A nearly-deaf man of Spruce Grove
Threw some dynamite into his stove;
The blast, heard for miles,
Left him wreathed all in smiles,
Cackling, "That wood really crackles, by Jove!"

A philandering husband of Standard
Grumbled, "Sure, I may well have meandered
- But that lawyer for my wife
Has made public my life,
And I feel I have truly been slandered."

Said a knotty centenarian of Stettler,
"I came into this district as a settler,
And havin' stuck it out
Through blizzard and drought,
I'll soon take my mortgage and settle 'er."

There once was a young man from Stirling
Who day and night spent his time curling.
It was not what you think;
He was not at the rink,
But a hair salon, tossing, teasing and twirling."

A modish fashion leader of Stony Plain
Wore thick makeup and flaunted a tony mane,
But an epiphany came
And she shed them in shame,
Still, she looks much the same - only plain.

Asked a somewhat slow student of Strathmore,
"What on earth would I ever learn math for?
Why, my brain might implode
- Or even explode;
Should I value my brain or some math more?"

A courageous young fellow of Stavely,
Who faces up to all challenges bravely,
Vows, "I shall continue to dine
On poutine and wine,
Though I well know this lust may enslave me."

A concerned old soul living near Suffield
Peered dolefully out on a rough field:
"A huge mess it is, thanks
To those bloody big tanks;
I hope the Army figures it has enough field."

A nervous young fellow of Sundre
Would panic when the weather was thundery,
And bad weather reports
Brought a quick change of shorts…
Which, on hand, he would always keep sundry.

A creative young lady of Sunnynook,
Presented a cheerful and sunny look,
But since she would wear
Live birds in her hair,
She was met, most times, with a *funny* look.

There once was a girl of Swan Hills
Who was totally dependent on pills;
Pills used, of course,
To treat her sick horse,
And not as a source of some thrills.

Said a sage husband from Sylvan Lake
"A sound marriage must be *give* and *take*:
I *give* my wife all my pay,
She *takes* it away
And spends every damned dollar I make."

There was a young maiden of Taber
Whose morals we need not belabour;
Suffice it to say
She premised each day
On her credo, which was "Love thy neighbour."

Said a right-thinking merchant of Thorhild,
"It's my duty to keep this here store filled
With every sort of rifle -
In case you've a wife to stifle,
Or a friend to be cautioned - or killed."

Gushed a vain young maiden of Thorsby,
"Every boy here in Thorsby adores me!
Though all seek my affection,
The fear of rejection
Is the reason that each one ignores me."

An old hypochondriac of Three Hills
Found his medical plan gave him free pills,
Which he downed in such number
He has found eternal slumber
In the cemetery 'neath one of those wee hills.

An untidy old-timer of Tilly
Said, "My taking a bath would be silly
… Or to change underwear
… Or run a comb through my hair,
Why, I'd simply be gilding the lily."

Said a thoughtful old farmer of Tofield,
"Half the year my whole farm's just a snowfield,
And when the snow goes, of course,
I must work like a horse…
Why, I think I would rather have no field."

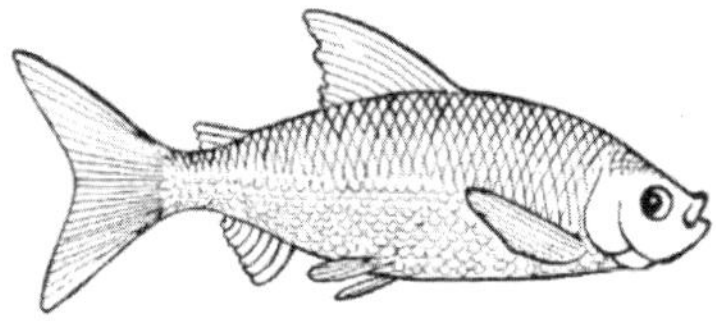

Said a camp cook up at Tulliby Lake,
" I use tullibee, of course, when I make
Tullibee soup, tullibee fillet,
Tullibee stew, tullibee skillet,
Tullibee bake, tullibee steak... and tullibee cake."

A disinterested father from Torrington
Was listening to his dull and boring son:
"There's these new gophers in the gopher museum,
Pa, you just gotta go in there and see 'em..."
But Pa was now getting some snoring done.

A dance student from Turner Valley
Feared her knees were turning to jelly,
As day after day
She practised her plié
- She was bent on improving her ballet.

A fellow who moved into Two Hills
Said, "I moved here simply to view hills,
And though two isn't many,
Where I was there weren't any
- And I've heard we're expecting some new hills."

A popular girl of Twin Butte
Was the subject of endless dispute:
Was her social success
Due to manners and dress?
… Or because she was just so darned cute?

A sawed-off young cowboy from Vauxhall
- Too short to see over a stock stall -
Received boots, as a gift,
With a 14-inch lift,
And today that young cow-puncher walks tall.

A politician campaigning in Valleyview
Told a crowd, "I've come here to rally you
To end - with great haste -
All government waste!"
But they knew it was just so much ballyhoo.

An old woman, Vera, of Vegreville,
One morning arose and felt vaguely ill,
So she doctored herself
With some pills from a shelf.
Last week they probated Vera’s will.

A lawyer who lived in Vermillion
Beamed, “I guess I’m just one-in-a-million,
Honest and warm,
And oozing with charm,”
But folks found him rather reptilian.

There was an old farmer of Veteran
Who shovelled feed grain ’til the sweat ran,
Then collapsed and, half dead,
Moaned, “Who can Help?” His wife said,
“I’ll phone and find out if the vet can.”

A contrary Scot, with a pottery in Vilna,
One morning, bright and early, gave his kiln a
Firing - one so hot
He could fire a large pot.
But would he? He declared, “Nay, I will na’.”

"The Lord," cried a preacher of Viking,
"Provides sights that are much to our liking;
And one I like best
Is to look down the chest
Of some young lady bent over biking."

"Play a V.L.T.?" mused a venerable sage of Vulcan,
"Why anyone with a brain in his skull can:
You just shove your coins in -
But to think you can win?
Well, there's something just the mentally dull can."

A wicked young wastrel from Wabamun
Decided one day he would rob a nun.
She had cash in her habit,
But before he could grab it
She had used her huge rosary to club him one.

A heavy toker of Wabasca-Desmerais,
Said, "I seem to know less day by day,
Which I ought to regret,
But somehow forget...
...Now what was I trying to say?"

An amateur boxer from Wainwright
Would not take the trouble to train right
And broke his nose in a bout
- Which was soon straightened out -
But they never could quite get his brain right.

A drunk uncle at a wedding in Walsh
Asked a bridesmaid, "Would you care to waltz?"
Then he stumbled and fell,
Lost his teeth, but said, "Well…
It's a good *fing*… them *teef*… are all… *falsh*."

Said a civic promoter of Warberg,
"This town ain't your '*only-one-store*' burg;
We got our gas co-op
And that big truck stop,
… I bet you ain't got neither in your burg."

A horse-loving lady of Warspite
Once suffered a serious horse-bite
When her steed, in a snit,
Was annoyed by it's bit:
- That poor woman was a victim of horse spite.

While dining with her beau in Watino
A girl, breaking wind, thought, "Does he know?"
He raised his brow slightly,
Then asked, quite politely,
"Ever consider cooking with *Beano*?"

A prolific old patriarch of Wembley,
Having summoned a family assembly,
Was heard to complain
To his wife, "Please explain
Why none of these children resemble me."

A rambling old barfly of Westlock
Kept babbling, "*Yale* makes the best lock;
Why, whenever I was in jail
All them cell locks was *Yale*....."
... But then no one would let the old pest talk.

A hospitable old man of Wetaskiwin,
If you ever dropped by, would ask you in
For a game of gin rummy,
Though he played like a dummy
And invariably conceded, "Alas, you win."

A toothless old codger of Wrentham
Chewed so hard on his dentures he bent them,
But chortled, "That harm
Ain't no cause for alarm;
I don't actually own them - I rent them."

A flaccid young fellow of Whitecourt
Resolved he would take up some light sport.
He decided on tennis,
But was seen as a menace,
Since he couldn't keep his balls on the right court.

Chirped a little old lady of Wildwood,
"I've lived in this town since my childhood,
And though a man who drinks beer
Says he'd like to move here,
I don't see how some person that wild could."

Sighed a self-effacing maiden of Worsely,
"Every boy here in Worsely abhors me.
Sure, I've heard some boys like me,
But the odds seem unlikely
- Although many do favours for me."

A youthful young redhead from Youngstown
Wore her tresses so long they hung down
Almost to her skirt
Guys would shout, "Red Alert!"
Hoping to flirt with that redhead of Youngstown.

There once was a man from Alberta
Who took a trip on a ship to Bizerte
... Which is apropos
To nothing - we know -
But there's not a lot rhymes with 'Alberta'.